The PRICE of POWER

DR. D. K. OLUKOYA

THE PRICE OF POWER

© 2016 DR. D. K. OLUKOYA

ISBN: 978-978-920-131-0

Published Feb, 2017

Published by:
The Battle Cry Christian Ministries
322, Herbert Macaulay Street, Sabo, Yaba
P. O. Box 12272, Ikeja, Lagos.
www.battlecrystores.com
email: info@battlecrystores.com
  customercare@battlecrystores.com
  sales@battlecrystores.com
Phone: 0803-304-4239, 0816-122-9775

I salute my wonderful wife, Pastor Shade, for her invaluable support in the ministry.
I appreciate her unquantifiable support in the book ministry as the cover designer, art editor and art adviser.

All the Scriptures are from the King James Version

All rights reserved. Reproduction in whole or part without a written permission is prohibited. Printed in Nigeria.

CONTENTS

CHAPTER		PAGE
1.	THE PRICE OF POWER	4
2.	SECRETS OF SPIRITUAL POWER	20
3.	CHURCH IN THE GRAVE	39
4.	CHALLENGES	49
5.	DEAD OR ALIVE	54
6.	EXAMINE YOURSELF	63

CHAPTER 1

THE PRICE OF POWER

If you do not want to be wasted, then, you must be concerned about the power content of your inner man. It is an insult on your salvation for local witchcraft, magicians, and satanic agents to manipulate you. It is an assault to God, that you can be arrested, through incantations and enchantments.

A woman came for prayers many years ago. This woman was a celebrity. Somebody entered into her shop, and demanded how much she had sold. She told him, the person demanded for the money, and she gave him. The person again asked for the most expensive thing she had in the shop. She told him, and the stranger asked her to bring it, too, she did. The person told the madam further, "I love this attire, how much did you buy it?" She told him. After that the person said, "Madam I would not like to disgrace you, but you can just take the wrapper, while you give me the blouse." The woman agreed, and gave him, her blouse. Then, he said, "Bye-bye," and,, walked away.

When her eyes got cleared, she started screaming, and started to read Psalm 23. But, how come, that the shepherd ran away, when a dubious person met her in the shop? Then, I asked, "Madam do you want to change your focus?" I told her the most important thing is, how powerful the inner man is. No matter the way the flesh is polished, one day somebody will say, ashes for ashes, dust for dust," and that is the truth. Are you there, buying special creams for your body, while the enemy is still pursuing you in the dream? You must retrace your steps.

It is compulsory for us to have adequate power, deposited in the inner man. We ought to be going from strength to strength, not from strength to weakness. Therefore, what is needed these days, is power from above, as opposed to powerlessness.

POWER ENCOUNTER

I was invited to a ministers' conference, and I declared, "Oh that God will bless this country, with just five Elijah's". If there are five Elijah's in this country, there would be perfect peace in the nation. If a community decides to fight, and one of such Elijah says, "You must not fight." If the prophet should say "Because you have insisted that you must fight, then, let fire come down." By that act, the evil intentions of people shall be brought to a halt. When power faces power, then, weaker power will pack up. When power faces power, one power will always supersede. One power must give way for the other. The Bible says, "evil men and seducers shall wax stronger and stronger."

If you take a cursory look at Acts 19, you will discover, that the people of Ephesus were keenly interested in witchcraft. These people of Ephesus were very much like the people of Nigeria today. Young men are using demonic powder to attract ladies. Some people bury something in the cemetery for seven days, after which they will take the thing back and put it in their pockets. People kidnap others, because they want money. Some take a bath, with blood everyday. There are people, who walk to market places, where there is crowd to test "juju" on people. All kinds of things are happening.

There are satanic agents, parading themselves all over the place. These were the occurrence in the biblical Ephesus, until the power of God arrested the situation.

HUMAN FOCUS

If the kind of power God has destined for His children, are in constant use by His children, they would become a terror in the kingdom of darkness. And, when you speak, your words shall carry weight. But, unfortunately, our lack of power in this generation has become rampant. We have concentrated our efforts on attachment, on make-ups and wearing clothes, that expose nakedness. We concentrate our efforts in wrong places. That is exactly, what the enemy wants. Because we focus our attention to a wrong direction. Several evil things have started coming forth in our midst.

THE PRICE OF POWER

Sisters, who are supposed to be prophetess of the Lord, cannot even hear a thing from God. There are some, with whom God wants to be discussing, but He has refused talking to them, because of the idol of jewelry. Men are coming to God's house, but they lack God's power. The reason for this is, that we are wrongly focused.

If you are powerless, then, you will become a chewing stick, in the mouth of powers of darkness. But, the mystery of it all, is that, such an evil man could, then, be forgiven after relinquishing his evil power. God may accept the evil man, whereas, the victims he had killed were wasted. Do you want to be wasted?

LEVELS OF POWER

There are four power levels in the spirit, or four energy levels in the spirit, and everybody belongs to one of these power levels. It is left for you to decide which of the power levels you desire.

1. Delegated spiritual authority – This power is not residence in the operator. It is just delegated. This power belongs to another person, and it is usually given, because of association with the owner of such power. As soon as a person is born again, certain amount of power is deposited into his spirit. He begins to tread upon serpents and scorpions, and they will not harm him. (Luke 10:19). Every believer has this at salvation. The delegated spiritual authority is the lowest spiritual energy level, in the kingdom.

2. **Authority, or Power** - Authority is different from power. If a policeman dressed in uniform, and stood at the road junction, saw a trailer coming, and raises his hand for the trailer to stop, the driver will stop the long vehicle, based on the authority invested on him. Such person dressed in police uniform, could even ask the driver to come down, and he would do exactly that, because of the authority that government has invested in the police force. The driver may be more muscular than the police man, in such that he will break the policeman into pieces, if allowed to fight one on one. The driver will never do so, because of the invested authority on the policeman.

THE REGALIA OF AUTHORITY

If the police officer has retired from service, and has dropped his uniform, and is moving in civilian attires. If, on a particular day, he puts on a flowing garment (Agbada), and steps at the junction to stop a trailer, ask the driver to come down, people will ask whether he is mad.

The power, which the policeman has, belong to the government, and not his own. The power government has is to punish anybody, who disobeys the policemen. If the policemen ask a vehicle to stop, but refuses to stop, then the owner of the authority vested on the policeman, has the power to punish the offender. There are some traffic warders in Nigeria, some are called 'yellow fever', because of their uniform, they could ask the vehicle to stop. I had seen people fighting these traffic controllers, because the authority vested on them were not enough to prevent them from being attacked.

> *"And the devil said unto him, If thou be the Son of God, command this stone that it be made bread."* Luke 4:3

There is difference between authority and power. The day you backslide like the policeman, who put down his uniform because he was retired, or you turn back on God, that authority would be taken away. A vast majority of believers operate on this level. There is a need to move forward.

2. **The Power of the Holy Spirit** – The second level of power, or energy level, is what is called, the power of the Holy Spirit.

> *"But ye shall receive power, after that the Holy Ghost is come upon you: and ye shall be witnesses unto me both in Jerusalem, and in all Judea, and in Samaria, and unto the uttermost part of the earth."*
> Acts 1:8

When you get baptised in the Holy Ghost, then, you have got something higher than the delegated authority. Any Christian, who is not filled with the

Holy Ghost, is missing a lot. If you cannot pray in tongues, then, the enemy will overpower you. You must be filled with the power of the Holy Ghost, with the evidence of speaking in tongues. The Bible says, "These signs shall follow them that believe, in my name they shall cast out devils; they shall speak with new tongues ..." That sign is for you, too.

If you have not received the baptism of the Holy Spirit, your power remains as delegated authority. That first level of power is not enough to handle African household witchcraft, let alone ancestral power. When anybody is praying in the spirit, speaking in tongues, then, he is charging his batteries.

> *"For he that speaketh in an unknown tongue speaketh not unto men, but unto God: for no man understandeth him; howbeit in the spirit he speaketh mysteries."*
> 1 Corinthians 14:2

When you are praying in tongues, you are speaking mystery.

> *"I thank my God, I speak with tongues more than ye all:"*
> 1 Corinthians 14:18

You have resident spiritual power, by consistently praying in tongues. The enemy will waste any person, who is not baptised in the Holy Ghost.

3. **Accumulated Spiritual Energy**- The third level of spiritual power is called, accumulated spiritual energy.

This is as a result of consistent and prolonged prayer and fasting. I am not talking of fasting that is not meaningful. God wants us to live a fasted life. God is happy with a fasted life, rather than, the almighty formula we are involved in. Some are still struggling with one day fasting, while God would have us go through more than three days fasting, without food, day and night. When there is no power, disappointment, frustration will set in.

THE POWERLESS PASTOR

There was a man, many years ago, who used to boast saying, "I am a powerful pastor." He always troubled General Overseer, saying, "Send me out, I want to demonstrate power?" He was, then, posted to a particular occult village. As he was in the village, one day, he went to ease himself in another man's farm. The farmer saw him, took a cutlass and sneaked to his back, and with the flattened part of the cutlass, he slapped his back. The farmer asked, "Why are you defecating in my farm?" When this man stood up, he told the farmer, "You beat up a man of God. In the next seven days, you will die." The farmer was really afraid. After seven days, when the farmer did not die, he went back to the pastor and said, "Man of God, I am still alive." Here was a man, who was boasting, "I want to explode!" But, he had no power. If it was another pastor with higher level of anointing, his pronouncement would come to pass.

If you want to be special for God, with the urge of helping others, the first energy level of power is not enough. When the mountain refuses to move and the powers of the devil are showing resistance, this is an indication, that the higher energy level is needed. But, there is a price to pay, which once paid, nothing shall be impossible. Elijah fasted for forty days, Moses fasted for forty days. Jesus himself fasted for forty days. They had accumulated spiritual energy.

4. **Dominion Level** – The fourth level, which is the last power level, is called, Dominion. This is the kind of power God gave to man, originally, in the Garden of Eden. Joshua exercised this power, when he asked the sun to stand still. Joshua did not get there in one day. He had been passing through different kinds of energy levels, until he reached the highest level of dominion. Moses talked to the earth and the earth obeyed, instantly. When you are a man of dominion, then, you will be bombarded with signs and wonders.

What shall we do to get to this level? This can be summarised with 4Ds.

(i)   Desire - Do you have strong desire to be strong?

THE PRICE OF POWER

(ii) Decision – Have you decided that you will be strong?

(iii) Determination – Are you determined, that at whatever cost, you will reach the highest level of power?

(iv) Discipline – No power without discipline.

When I was in the University of Lagos several years ago, I was young, then. Most of the older undergraduates decided to pass at all costs. These older people, decided to have a degree. They put in their best to succeed. One night, I was in the classroom reading, when I saw an old man struggling to pass. He did something very strange and difficult, for him to keep awake. He brought a bucket of water, and dropped some ice inside, puts his legs inside, and was reading. That is what we call discipline.

Things cannot be going down in your life, when your power is increasing. When the power level is higher, then, you can make circumstances change,

Jesus spoke to a tree, he spoke to the wind, he spoke to the dead bodies, he spoke to adverse situations, and they all obeyed him, because He possessed the highest spiritual level of power. The Bible says, God created all things, and put them under mankind. You must rediscover this level of dominion today.

PRAYER POINTS

1. Thou power of God, incubate my life, in the name of Jesus.
2. Power that cannot be insulted by the power of darkness, fall upon my life, in the name of Jesus.
3. My words be charged with the fire of God, in the name of Jesus.
4. Fire of God, come upon my life, in the name of Jesus.
5. Dominion power, come upon my life, in the name of Jesus.

6. Mantle of powerlessness in my life, catch fire in Jesus name.
7. I de-enroll myself from the school of powerlessness in the name of Jesus.
8. Let the hunger and thirst for the kingdom of God and righteousness possess my life in the name of Jesus.
9. Covenants from my foundation speaking weakness into my spiritual life, be destroyed in Jesus' name.
10. I receive large appetite for the word of God and holiness in the name of Jesus.
11. Let all multiple strongmen operating against me, be paralysed, in Jesus' name.
12. Lord, open my eyes and ears, to receive wondrous things from you, in the name of Jesus.
13. Lord, grant me victory over every temptation and satanic device in Jesus' name.

14. Lord, ignite my spiritual life, so that I will stop fishing in unprofitable waters, in Jesus name.
15. Lord, release the Pentecostal tongue of fire to burn in my life, in the name of Jesus.

CHAPTER 2

SECRETS OF SPIRITUAL POWER

God wants us to charge our batteries. The ingredients that will keep our batteries charged, are known as spiritual hunger and thirst. Two things you must never lack in your spiritual life, are hunger and thirst. Immediately, they are gone from your life, forget it. It is a nice thing, when you feel hungry to pray, read the word of God, or hear the word of God. It is a feeling of demotion, when you lose interest in these things.

If you want fire to remain in your life, without this hunger and thirst, is like players gathering on a football pitch, without a ball. The players cannot play any game. Hunger is the football in the football pitch, without it, there is no game. "Blessed are those that thirst and hunger after righteousness, for they shall be filled." It is time for many of us to pray, that the snail anointing should get out of our spiritual lives.

LAZY CHRISTIANS

Sometime ago, in England, I preached the gospel and ministered to an English boy. I spoke to him on a Tuesday, and by the time we met again the following Tuesday for another meeting, this boy of about 17, had read through the whole Bible for the first time. He sat down, and read the Bible, through in one week.

There are many people, who have been born again for many years, but, yet, to read through the New Testament. Some people start, only to give up half way. Some have been saying, "Well, I will make sure that on weekends I keep my programme low, so that I can be alone with God, pray, fast and read the word of God." They boasted and started off only to give up by the third week. Such people cannot hope to charge their batteries.

CONSTANT HUNGER

Do you want to receive great power from God? Then, this hunger is a must; there is no two ways to it. Hunger for God, is one of the greatest signs of spiritual people. Why is it that some people can

THE PRICE OF POWER

pray for three, or four hours non stop? It is, because there is something inside their lives. When a person can read the whole of the book of Matthew at a sitting, there is something special inside the life of such a person. It is not possible to climb a spiritual mountain, without any discipline. It is not possible for you to receive power, without consecration.

Out of all the spiritual gifts in the Bible, the one that you see easily in people's lives is prophecy. There are very few people in other areas, because not many people are ready to consecrate themselves, and drop a few things, so that they can gain the power of God. It is very sad, that true and powerful men of God are reducing in number. Women are, even, a lot lower in number, and this is very sad.

Unless we, as an end-time church, decides to pick up the mantle, determine that we must affect our own generation positively, God will blame us for allowing evil things to happen. Do you want this great power? Hunger is a must.

No matter how intelligent a person is, it will be very difficult for him to switch on his torchlight in the dark, when the batteries are dead.

If the batteries inside your torchlight have rusted and old, although you may have a new bulb, you will still have a problem, because you need power, which comes from the batteries to run the bulb.

> *"Blessed are they which do hunger and thirst after righteousness: for they shall be filled."* Matthew 5:6

Notice the strong phrase: 'they shall be filled.' That is, without fail, it must happen. In that passage we can see that the condition for being filled is to hunger, and thirst after righteousness. The Bible says, that those, who fulfill this condition, shall be filled.

> *"And ye shall seek me, and find me, when ye shall search for me with all your heart."* Jeremiah 29: 13

THE PRICE OF POWER

God is asking for 100 per cent of your heart.

> *"Blessed are ye that hunger now: for ye shall be filled."* Luke 6: 21

This is repeating, what we read in Matthew 5: 6. In John 7: 37, a spectacular thing happened. Normally, Jesus does not raise His voice, but in this verse, He did. Wherever you read about Jesus raising His voice in the Scriptures, know that it must be a very serious matter.

> *"In the last day, that great day of the feast, Jesus stood and cried, saying, if any man thirst, let him come unto me and drink."* John 7: 37

Please, raise your voice, and pray like this: "I drink now from the well of salvation, in Jesus' name.

From the four Scriptures we have read, we can see the key to charging our spiritual batteries. The Bible says, that in the last days, men shall become lovers of money, lovers of themselves, and that they would love pleasures more than God. It also says, there would be a lot of uproar and evil men shall wax stronger and stronger. So, we, as believers, cannot afford to sit down and be rejoicing, about what happened yesterday, or last year, or about how we prophesied the other time. We must continually charge our batteries. Our spiritual batteries have to be on fire.

Thousands of people come to the house of God, listen to the word of God, pray the prayers, come to all the services, join the groups, but remain unchanged. Some have already made up their minds on what to do, before coming to church. They pick and choose from the messages. When you come to God like that, He would turn His face away. God does not want people who have made up their minds. He wants people He can mould, into what He wants.

Have you ever decided on your own, to fast and pray for days, just to be with God, and for His power to fall upon your life, not because of problems? A certain man said, that when somebody is hungry, he would not find any fault with the food. He would forget whether there is salt or none. It is only when a person is not hungry, that he begins to complain, about the food. When you are hungry for God like that, the hunger drives you closer to God.

Any serious Christian must have at least one, or two days in the week, for fasting and praying. The reasons you need to do this, is to charge your batteries, and get your cup filled over and over. Somebody asked a great preacher called, D. L. Moody the following question: "Mr. Moody, why are you always talking about being filled, and filled with the Holy Spirit?" Mr. Moody answered thus: "I always talk about us being filled and filled, because we all leak and have to be re-filling and re-filling." The power of God will manifest in your life all the time, and the enemy cannot catch you unawares when you keep charging your batteries.

DEVIL'S AGENDA

The devil is catching many Christians unawares because they are not charging their batteries. It is commonly said that when fire has gone from the cooking place, all kinds of insects and reptiles will have the confidence to go there. But when you have red-hot fire at the cooking place, it will be very difficult for a lizard to come near it. It is not possible.

A hungry man would learn something, no matter, who is preaching. It can be so sad for people to come before God, and leave the same way they came. I pray that the Lord will open up our understanding, in Jesus' name.

> *"I love them that love me; and those that seek me early shall find me."* Proverbs 8: 17

Many start to seek the Lord at old age. Many always think that there is time, and a lot of people do not bother about God, until they go to the cemetery. The above Scripture is saying, that the time to seek God is now. Now is the time to be hungry for God, not when you are older; not when you can no longer stand and pray for two hours.

Some people feel, that they have sufficient time to play around a little bit, and be serious later. There is no time to be serious later, the time is now because you do not know, when your time here would be up. All the excuses of, "I am so busy in the office; my schedule is so tight, etc" will be useless. How sad it would be for you to tell the Lord, that you spent all your life working in one office, or reading Physics on the day of reckoning!

WHAT IS THE PROBLEM OF PRESENT DAY CHRISTIANS?

Is sin our problem? No. The Apostles, too, were not perfect people. Is our problem insufficient quantity of the Holy Spirit? No. We have the same Holy Spirit, as they had. Is our problem civilization? No, because it is actually Christianity that brought about civilization. Is it economic problem? No. The Bible says, "The earth is the Lord's and the fullness thereof."

The problem is lack of hunger. The present-day Christians are not thirsty after God. The Lord picked up Peter, who was fishing and catching nothing. And after Jesus picked him up, He said to him," "I will make you fishers of men." So, God's purpose for the life of Peter was to be a fisher of men. But, the same Peter ran away in John 21 to do something else, the very thing which he was delivered, originally.

ON FIRE FOR GOD

A certain little boy, who was hungry after God, asked his father, "Daddy, what would I do to be on fire for God, continually?" His father asked, if he really meant what he was saying, and the boy said, "yes". His father, then, took him to a small pond. Immediately they got there, his father bounced on him, and pushed his head underneath the water.

The boy began to struggle for air, and as he was doing that, he was gulping water. At the third gulp, his father then released him, and asked: "What did you desire most, when I dipped your head inside the water?" The boy said, "Fresh air," and the father said, "When you are hungry and thirsty after God, like the way you thirsted for air now, fire will fall upon your life." Beloved, that is it.

THE PRICE OF POWER

Our aim should be for God, to use us to cause a supernatural revival of apostolic signs and wonders. The apostles moved in the supernatural. They cast down strongholds, uprooted demonic trees, trampled upon satanic powers, worked earth-shaking miracles, turned cities upside down for Jesus, burned demonic materials, and God used them to lay the foundation for what we are enjoying now.

What is causing our lack of hunger for the Lord these days, can be found in the question Jesus asked Peter in John 21: 15 and which says,

> *"So when they had dined, Jesus saith to Simon Peter, Simon, son of Jonas, lovest thou me more than these? He saith unto him, Yea, Lord; thou knowest that I love thee. He saith unto him, Feed my lambs. He saith to him again the second time, Simon, son of Jonas, lovest thou me? He saith unto him, Yea, Lord; thou*

> *knowest that I love thee. He saith unto him, Feed my sheep. He saith unto him the third time, Simon, son of Jonas, lovest thou me? Peter was grieved because he said unto him the third time, Lovest thou me? And he said unto him, Lord, thou knowest all things; thou knowest that I love thee. Jesus saith unto him, Feed my sheep."* John 21:15-17

Peter failed at a profession in, which he was an expert. Many, too, are failing woefully today, at what they know how to do, because of lack of the hunger for Jesus in them. Jesus asked Peter, if he loved Him more than all the disciples, more than his boats and more than his fishing. Today, He is asking you the same question.

SELF EXAMINATION

Do you love Jesus more than the world? Do you love Jesus more than all the glamorous things, that are around you? Are you the kind of person, who would abandon fellowship, because you want to go to a worldly party? Do you love Jesus? It is the love for Him, that will create the hunger.

A careful consideration of the following questions, will help you to test your level of spiritual hunger for the Lord. Have you forgiven everyone, who has offended you? Is there any malice, or hatred in your heart? Another year is going now, and God is putting everything on record. Do you cherish grudges in your heart? Have you refused to be reconciled with somebody you quarreled with? Do you get angry? Do you still lose your temper? Or, do you boil internally? Do you get jealous? Is envy in your heart?

Are you sweet and clean under heavy pressure, or circumstances? Are you easily offended? Does it hurt you, when somebody ignores you? Are you disturbed, when you are neglected? Is there pride in your heart? Do you always like to be noticed?

Are you always dishonest, when it comes to money? Do you gossip about people? Do you discuss other people behind their backs, in a negative way?

Are you on assignment for Jesus? Do you obey Him all the time? Do you steal, particularly God's money? Would the people of the world regard you as being different from them? It is sad when an unbeliever looks at a Christian and what he or she likes about the Christian is her kind of lipstick and finger nails polish, instead of the holiness and righteousness of God in your life.

Such a Christian is advertising vanity, instead of God. The person has become like Hezekiah, who, when some people came to visit him, he took them around, showed them the beauty of the temple and they left. Then, God asked him, "Hezekiah, what have they found in your house?" He could not talk. God said, "You advertised to them all the decorations and beauty, but you refused to talk to them about the God of Israel, that added 15 years to your life. Should that not be the first thing to talk to them about?" God had to deal with him.

FOR THE LOVE OF CHRIST

Peter got arrested and locked up somewhere in Rome. As the soldiers were going to kill him, he escaped, when he had the opportunity to do so. On his way out, he met Jesus and asked Him, "Lord where are you going?" Jesus replied, "To go and die for you the second time." When Peter heard that, he walked back with his own legs to the Prison, from which he had escaped, because he remembered the words of the Lord to him; Do you love me? Feed my sheep."

He went back and they promptly caught him. As they were going to crucify him, he said, Sirs, do not crucify me the way you crucified Jesus." So, they turned Peter upside down, and crucified him. That was how he died, because he loved Jesus. The Bible says, "And they loved not their lives unto death." The reason some people are afraid of death is, because they do not love Jesus. When you love Jesus, and the devil sees that you are no longer afraid of death, he will run away from you.

Have you wronged anyone, and you do not want to make restitution? Are you a spiritual-yes person? Do you receive anything from the Holy Spirit? Have you received the spirit of Zachaeus? Do you steal spoons, beds, chairs, office equipment, etc, from hotels and offices? Are you an extortionist? These are the things that kill spiritual fire. Are you a fornicator, or an adulterer? Do you get anxious, or worried about any small thing?

Do you pretend to have forgiven somebody, when you have not really forgiven the person? Do you disobey men of God? Are you guilty of immorality in the heart? Do you harbour in-pure, or unholy imaginations? Are you the kind of person, who exaggerates? Do you tell lies to cover up your faults? Do you pray for others? Are you guilty of the sin of prayerlessness? Are you neglecting the Bible?

How many chapters a day, of the Bible, do you read? Do you witness about Jesus to people? Do you have compassion in your heart for souls, that are perishing? Have you lost your first love for the

Lord? How can a person planning for heaven buy a tie worth N20,000, whereas he cannot spend N5,000 to buy and distribute tracts to people, so that they can, at least, enjoy the benefits of Jesus?

Do you attend parties of unbelievers, looking around, hoping that nobody from your church is there to see you. Because, if they see you, you would be used to preach the following Sunday, you stayed in the dark areas? These are the ways to check the level of your hunger for the Lord. Beloved, think about these things.

PRAYER POINTS

1. O Lord, forgive me for not opening enough room to the Holy Spirit, in the name of Jesus.

2. All spiritual blockages in my life, be cleared out by the Blood of Jesus.

3. Anything contrary to the Holy Spirit in my life, be cleared out by fire, in the name of Jesus.

4. Lord, increase in my life and help me to crucify flesh, in the name of Jesus.
5. You spirit of failure in my life, depart, in the name of Jesus.
6. You spirit of weakness in my life, depart, in the name of Jesus.
7. You quenchers of power in my life, die, in the name of Jesus.
8. Every enemy of prayer in my life, release me, in the name of Jesus
9. Lord, give me the spmt that prays without ceasing, in the name of Jesus.
10. I shall not fail in my prayer life, in the name of Jesus.
11. Father Lord, tech me to die to self in the name of Jesus.
12. I stand against loss of focus in my walk with God in the name of Jesus.
13. I sack spiritual laziness from every department of my life in Jesus name.

14. O Lord let the hunger and thirst for the kingdom of God and righteousness possess my life in Jesus' name.
15. Mantle of power and fire from the Holy of Holies fall upon me in the name of Jesus.
16. I call forth new patterns of grace upon my life in Jesus' name.
17. Let the lust of the flesh, lust of the eyes and pride of life die in my life in Jesus' name.
18. I disconnect all works of the flesh from my life in Jesus' name.
19. Strange fire burning in my members be quenched in the name of Jesus.
20. Holy Ghost arise and infuse fresh fire into my life in Jesus' name.

CHAPTER 3
CHURCH IN THE GRAVE

The content of this chapter may indeed seem strange to you. It may set you wondering about, the existence of a church in the graveyard. You may, then, wish to ask, or, perhaps, to establish the differences between a church and a graveyard.

The church, as you know it, is a place of worship for the living, while the graveyard is the final resting place for the physically dead. It, then, follows, that if a church is to be built in a graveyard, no activity will take place therein.

In order to understand this message, I beseech you to, prayerfully, read through. Open your heart, and the proper digestion of the message will give you understanding, in Jesus name. Amen.

THE PRICE OF POWER

Our Bible passage shall be taken from Revelation chapter 3 verses 1 to 6. Please, take note, that the book of revelation was written by Apostle John, and was addressed to the seven churches in Asia. Three of those churches, were addressed in Chapter three. It reads thus.

> *"And unto the angel of the church in Sardis write; These things saith he that hath the seven Spirits of God, and the seven stars; I know thy works, that thou hast a name that thou livest, and art dead Be watchful, and strengthen the things which remain, that are ready to die: for I have not found thy works perfect before God Remember therefore how thou hast received and heard, and hold fast, and repent. If therefore thou shalt not watch, I will come on thee as a thief, and*

> *thou shalt not know what hour I will come upon thee Thou hast a few names even in Sardis, which have not defiled their garments; and they shall walk with me in white: for they are worthy He that overcometh, the same shall be clothed in white raiment; and I will not blot out his name out of the book of life, but I will confess his name before my Father, and before his angels, He that hath an ear, let him hear what the Spirit saith unto the churches".* Rev 3:1-6.

Verses one to six were particularly addressed to the church in Sardis. The Bible says, that the church had a name. But, as far as God was concerned, that church was dead.

YOUR STATUS

When you look at this fact very closely, you will find out that, it is not what you call yourself, that actually matters, but what God calls you. It is possible for you to call yourself double apostle, or even angel, but as far as God is concerned, He thinks differently about you. The Lord said, that that church once had a name, but was dead thereafter. It follows that it would no longer function as it used to be. A dead person will behave like the dead, and a living person as the living. While some people in the churches today, are spiritually awake, others are spiritually dead. The latter, are those the Bible refers to, as dead people.

A quick look at the word of God will tell you, that the Bible talks about five groups of spiritually dead people. If however, the Bible regards one as dead, and the person is regarding himself as living, then, such a person is deceiving himself, or herself. The groups of dead people are as follows.

The first groups of dead people are as follows:

1. THE BACKSLIDERS

They are those, who have stopped following the Lord the way He should be followed. They are people, whose spiritual lives are now very weak. Indeed, they are people, who find it difficult to pray and study the word of God. They find it difficult to witness to others about the Lord Jesus Christ. But, the Lord is now asking spiritual sleepers to stay awake. He is also challenging the spiritually dead people to rise up. It is certain, therefore, that backsliders are spiritual sleepers. As far as the Lord is concerned, they are dead.

2. SINNERS

All sinners are spiritually dead people. The day a sinner becomes alive, is the day that he repents from his sins, and cries for forgiveness. When that happens, such a sinner has become aware, that he was dead and needed to give his life to the Lord Jesus, to come alive. All sinners, as far as the Bible is concerned, are dead people.

3. THE CARNALLY MINDED PEOPLE

> Romans 8:6
> *"For to be carnally minded is death; but to be spiritually minded is life and peace".*

It follows therefore, that a person, who is always thinking of carnal things is dead while alive. Such a person is not interested in how you can grow spiritually. He or she is only interested in how to make more money and to become more comfortable. A carnal mind is an abomination to God, that is why the bible says that to be carnally minded is death.

4. THE HATERS OF KNOWLEDGE

The fourth group of dead people are found in the book of Proverbs 21:6

> *"The getting of treasures by a lying tongue is a vanity tossed to and fro of them that seek death".*

These are those, who are not interested in learning more about the Lord Jesus Christ. They are just comfortable, or contended with, how they are spiritually. Such people think they have got it all.

5. PLEASURE SEEKERS

The last group of spiritually dead people are found in

> 1 Tim. 5:6
> *"But she that liveth in pleasure is dead while she liveth".*

As far as the Bible is concerned, pleasure seekers today attend churches. They are only happy, when there are lots of singing and dancing and entertainment around. Dead people! As far as the Bible is concerned, they are not even qualified to praise God.

It is amazing that many have not known this fact, that the spiritually dead people are not qualified to praise the Lord.

> Psalm 115:17
> *"The dead praise not the Lord, neither any that go down into silence"*

The book of Isaiah 38:19

> ***"The living, the living, he shall praise thee, as I do this day: the father to the children shall make known thy truth".***

Thus, dead people are not qualified to praise God. Dead churches are not even qualified to praise the Lord, too. Such people should not even expect anything that will last from God! In fact the Bible says, that they are not even qualified to handle the word of God.

Beloved, I would like you to close your eyes, where you are now, and quietly examine your spirit.

Perhaps, you have been classifying yourself wrongly. Perhaps, you are not aware, that you are not in the classification of the Almighty God. Begin to talk to the Lord at this moment. Ask the Holy Spirit, to give you the true picture of your life today. Talk with the Lord now.

PRAYER POINTS

1. Any part of me thirsting for the things of the world, receive deliverance by fire in the name of Jesus.
2. O Lord, heal every form of backsliding in my life in the name of Jesus.
3. I rise out of the valley of sin to the mountain top of righteousness in the name of Jesus
4. Resurrection power of God, possess my body, soul and spirit in the name of Jesus.
6. I plug myself into the socket of power of the almighty God in the name of Jesus.
7. Garment of spiritual hindrance, garment of spiritual weakness in my life roast by fire in the name of Jesus.
8. Arrow of powerlessness, depart from my life in Jesus' name.
8. Certificate of the wasters in my hand, I set you ablaze in Jesus' name.
9. Fire of purification sanitize my heart in the name of Jesus.

10. Holy Spirit quicken me in every area of my life in Jesus' name.
11. My Father, deliver me today from besetting; sin, in the name of Jesus.
12. Every stranger in the dark room of my life, come out now! in the name of Jesus.
13. Every destructive habit, chasing heaven away from my heart, clear away! in the name of Jesus.
14. Every ladder of darkness, giving the enemy access to my life, clear away! in name of Jesus.
15. My Father, visit me! in the name of Jesus.
16. Anything planted in my life, to take me to hell fire, be uprooted by fire! in the name of Jesus.
17. Dead fish floats, I refuse to float, in the name of Jesus.
18. Garment of darkness, upon my spiritual body, tear away! in the name of Jesus.
19. Garment of shame and disgrace, catch fire and burn to ashes, in the name of Jesus.
20. Every power assigned to waste my life in hell fire, clear awa! in the name of Jesus.

CHAPTER 4
CHALLENGES

James the son of Zebedee, an apostle loved the Lord until his death. When he was going to be killed, he witnessed to the Roman soldiers, who were taking him away. The executor became interested, and when they got to where James was to be killed, the soldier said, "Sorry, you have to kill us together. I am not killing this man." His colleagues reported him. James did not die alone. He died with the soldier, that was meant to kill him. They loved not their lives unto death. Under harsh conditions, some Christians deny Jesus. This is very sad, indeed.

The reason masquerades and other demonic things are running after many people in their dreams is, because they are afraid of death. The apostles passed that level. They loved not their lives unto death. We read that Philip was dragged on the ground, until the whole of his clothes were torn terribly wounded, before he was nailed on the tree. Matthew was made to sit down and clubbed to death. They loved not their lives unto death. Stephen was stoned to death. Brother Andrew was crucified naked on a cross, with an 'X' shape. The man, who wrote the book of Mark in the Bible, was dragged on the ground before an idol, while he was preaching, until his flesh was torn into pieces. They loved not their lives unto death. Almost all the apostles died a terrible death, because of the gospel.

HOLY HUNGER

Are you hungry for Jesus? Is the hunger for God in you now higher, than what it was last year? Now that another year is coming, are you still at that same level of breaking down and crying, instead of standing your ground to fight the enemy? What, then, do we do now?

We need to pray seriously, that the Lord should close down, every factory of the enemy in our lives. It is from this factory, that anger and all kinds of evil things, are coming out. All satanic factories should be closed down, because their existence will entrench lack of hunger for God, and kill spiritual fire. We also need to pray, that the power of resurrection should enter into our lives afresh. When the power of resurrection of the Lord Jesus Christ comes upon you, you will not be afraid of anything, because, since Christ is still living in you, nobody can kill you. We also need to pray, that every spirit of death and hell should depart. The spirit of death and hell operates in two ways:

1. They sponsor untimely death.

2. They deposit people in hell fire.

We have to stand against them, so that the fire of revival will enter into our souls, and when this happens to us, you need not tell somebody, that God has done a miracle in your life. People will know, that something has happened to you.

You have to go to the mountain, where God wants you to be, and if, you need to be pushed, for you to get there, you shall be given the push. One practical way of getting started is, to get serious with your Bible study. Another practical way, is to decide to pray for a minimum of half an hour per day, and stick to it, no matter, what happens.

Please, pray the following prayer points with these four things: holy stubbornness, holy aggression, holy violence and stubborn faith.

PRAYER POINTS

1. Every factory of the enemy militating against me, fall down and die, in Jesus' name.
2. O Lord, send your resurrection power into my life, in the name of Jesus.
3. Every spirit of death and hell, my life is not your candidate, in the name of Jesus.
4. Every evil root growing in my family, be uprooted by fire, in the name of Jesus.
5. Inherited demotion, fall down and die, in the name of Jesus.
6. Every power sitting on my promotion, be unseated by fire, in the name of Jesus.

7. Every dark power, assigned to write the last chapter of my life, you are a liar, die, in the name of Jesus.
8. My Father, barricade my life from deception, in the name of Jesus.
9. Anything in my life, that is reducing my mark in heaven, clear away, in the name of Jesus.
10. Father Lord, give me oil in my lamp, and keep me burning for you now and forever more, in Jesus' mighty name.
11. Wicked yokes over my life break by fire in the name of Jesus.
12. I confront and conquer all levels of darkness contending with my star in the name of Jesus.
13. Higher power of Cod, rest upon my life in the name of Jesus.
14. Holy Ghost change' my identify to fire in the name of Jesus.

CHAPTER 5

DEAD OR ALIVE

I do hope, you have not forgotten a memorable story, which involves Paul in Acts Chapter16:16-19 While Paul was preaching the word of God in Philippians, a certain damsel, who had the spirit of divination from the devil, kept following him, prophesying, that Paul and his ministers were servants of the most high God, sent to preach salvation to the people. Although, she was saying the correct things, Paul, nonetheless, had to keep her quiet. The reason he did that, was to ensure that an unworthy vessel, possessed of satanic spirit does not speak the word of God. Little wonder then, that he rebuked the spirit in the girl, and commanded it to depart from her, right from that moment.

Know this fact, therefore, that the lady could not be allowed to handle the word of God because she was not spiritually fit.

THE PRICE OF POWER

Many people, stubbornly, sit tight in their dead churches, and many take solace in their dead environment. It is such places, that the household enemies will ensure that such people are given church posts, in order to tie them down. And they would never be able to attend a living church, where they would be saved. When such people are told to pray, they would start naming their church posts, instead of praying. The devil has, deceitfully, planted things in them. It is an evidence of life, not alive to God at all.

I need to tell you my story here. A long time ago, I was attending a very big church. I was an organist, as well as, a choirmaster of the church. The church bought a big organ practically because of me. The church was even indebted to the tune of ten thousand naira, because of the organ. They promised me heaven on earth, in that particular church. I resumed my choirmaster job in full, as soon as I returned from England. The turning point came, however, with a night vision.

THE STRONG MAN

One day in a night vision, I saw something terrible. I saw a tall black man, standing right at the middle of the church. All of us in the church, that were very prayerful, and who did not like the way things were going on, started fighting that tall black man with a horse whip. Each person had a horse whip in his hand. We were beating him with all our strength. But, the more we beat the man, the stronger he became. Then, at a stage, those of us who were beating him, conferred together on what to do. We reasoned that the more we beat this man the stronger he became.

We, then, concluded, that the man was the cause of the trouble in the whole church. As we conferred together in that vision, somebody observed that the black demon was not affected, because the horse-whip we were using was not effective. To confirm this, we decided to test the horse whip on the body of one of us. The horse whip was used to beat one of us, and blood started oozing out of his body. Then, the man we were fighting started laughing at us, that although, we came to fight him, we started fighting one another almost, immediately.

The voice of the Lord came to me in the vision very audibly, that He, the Lord, did not ask me to stay in that church. I left the church, immediately. Thereafter, about six of us started our fellowship meeting in a small shop. People laughed at me and in fact ridiculed me that, if I had read mathematics, they would have thought I was mad. They wondered how I could leave a big church, to fellowship in a small shop with six people.

But, I thank God that I did not listen to them at all. If I had listen to them, there would not have been MFM ministries today. What answer would I have given for the blood of many believers I would have on my head?
The lesson, here, is that taking up post in dead church is tantamount, to voting for the graveyard.

THE SHACKLE
Many people are tied down with church posts, which later turn them to cemetery place. I hope

you know this fact that, whatever effort a policeman puts in the burial ground to look after the dead, is a useless exercise.

They make people churchwarden of the dead, choirmaster for the dead, patron for the dead, matron for the dead etc. All such posts are to ensure the death of such people themselves.

If, somebody is spiritually dead, he does not see the way any longer. Such people may not know who they are until the Spirit of God departs from them.

I was going to a church before, where all we did on Sundays was to dance, clap our hands and sing, jumping on the benches. After we would have done all that, the Pastor would announce that our time was far spent, therefore, he would not be able to preach any sermon. But we had enough time for endless offerings. Thereafter, we would say the grace and go home. While we were busy doing that, the devil was not only rejoicing, but also planted endless calamities amidst us.

AN UNFORGETTABLE EXPERIENCE

I was going to that church, until one day, when something which shook me out of that condition happened to me. Somebody was boiling oil on fire and I was sitting nearby, reading my book.

Then something strange happened. Before my very eyes, the oil on fire became a ball, and travelled to my direction, and fell on my leg. I could not move at all, I cried out to the entire household for help. The first person, who came said, let us pour ice water on his legs, another person said, let us put pap, and another pleaded that they should put egg, while my leg was busy burning, they were busy arguing. Eventually, they agreed on what to do. I was, nonetheless, managing with one leg.

Then, within two months my left hand broke again. So, I had a broken hand and a roasted leg. Then, one night, the Lord came to me and warned me, that I would end up, being killed in the dead church I was attending. The Lord told me, that if, I had been attending a living church, I would have been able to reject calamities, that befell me.

It was at that time that I started calling on the name of the Lord the way it should be called. He heard me, and promoted me from my terrible spiritual position, to the top of the rock.

PRAYER POINTS

1. I wake up into my divine destiny, in the name of Jesus.
2. I refuse to die unfulfilled, in the name of Jesus.
3. I resist and conquer voice silencers in the name of Jesus.
4. The Lord has made me a divine pillar in my father's house, I manifest by fire in the name of Jesus.
5. Agenda of destiny miscarriage for my life die by fire in the name of Jesus.
6. Holy Spirit, activate divine power in every area of my life in Jesus' name.
7. Father Lord, teach me to dwell in your secret place in the name of Jesus.

THE PRICE OF POWER

8. I receive power; I receive fire that cannot be molested by any form of darkness in the name of Jesus.
9. Holy Ghost fireworks explode in my life in the name of Jesus.
10. Let my divine eagle arise and shine in the name of Jesus.
11. Thou power of limitation and stagnation in my life, hear the word of the Lord, die! in the name of Jesus.
12. Every strongman assigned against my project of prosperity, your time is up, therefore, die! in the name of Jesus.
13. My hands shall finish the project that they have started, in the name of Jesus.
14. Power to finish and to finish well, come upon my life! in the name of Jesus.
15. My project of prosperity, hear the word of the Lord: Arise and shine in the name of Jesus.
16. O heavens over my life, open by Fire! in the name of Jesus.

17. Every evil power, delegated to monitor and destroy me, die! in the name of Jesus.
18. Every evil padlock, working against any department of my life, break and roast to ashes! in the name of Jesus.
19. I shall become what God created me to be, in the name of Jesus.
20. All paralysed potentials and talents, receive the resurrection power of the Blood of Jesus Christ, in the name of Jesus.

CHAPTER 6

EXAMINE YOURSELF

The problem of the church today is the presence of many hypocrites. They have refused to leave their sins and their dead churches, the Lord cannot help such people.

You do not do the work of the Lord deceitfully, you cannot cheat God, if you do, you will pay for it.

If you hide your spiritual condition, God will leave you to your problems. If you are struggling to do some other things, that you are not supposed to do, then, you must wake up, for God is concerned about you.

If the trumpet of the Lord should sound today, the evidence that you are in good church is, that you will reign with Christ.

A lot of people are too worldly to be useful, spiritually. They are afraid, or ashamed of being tagged, fanatics for Jesus. But, the truth is that, that is what the Lord expects of you.

PERSONAL IDOLS

Many people do not want to serve the Lord, because of certain things in their lives, which they do not want to drop. They are afraid, that if, they join the Christian fold, they would not be able to do such things, that please them again. Those things have become idols to them. Anything at all, that you cannot drop for the sake of God, has become an idol in your life. All you want to do, is to please human beings.

When the time of rapture comes, these people you are seeking to please, will not be able to help you at all. They are totally useless, as far as spiritual help is concerned.

Why should you design your life, after the thoughts and the love of the people of the world? Why should a child of hell fire, decide your dress pattern for you? How could they be the ones to tell you whether, or not you are looking fine, or dull? Even, if you are looking dull, is that the business of a child of hell-fire? If they say, you are looking dull, and heaven says, you are looking bright, will you not be happy? Immediately you begin to live the type of life the Lord wants; you will invite enemies, automatically, to yourself. Nobody will have the guts to invite you to worldly parties again. The moment you are God crazy, even if, they had put your name unknowingly, they would, definitely, erase it.

You cannot be hot for God, without becoming automatic enemies of people of the world. It is a pity, however, that some people compromise their faith, to please people of darkness.

When somebody is dead spiritually, good things that are spiritually inclined will not be opened to him, or her.

A dead person cannot serve God, only a living person can.

When everything is almost gone, and all things are closing down, it is, then, many people will realise how much debts they owe to the Lord. Many of such people will realise the vanity of the world, in which their lives had been.

Each person will account individually for his, or her stewardship on earth, even, couples will account, individually. Therefore, you cannot blame your husband, wife, or children for your lack of spiritual development. If you seek pleasure alone, while you are alive, you are indeed dead

Why should believers follow unbelievers to their parties, and help them to do their cooking?

If you are still worshipping God in your sins, then, you are not in any way different from the dead church of the Sardis, a church that was in the burial ground.

Take a step of faith today, by separating yourself from the churches, or groups of the dead.

THE PRICE OF POWER

Separate yourself in your mode of dressing, conversation, attitude, faith, way of life etc.

Quit from the congregation of the dead people today. It, really, does not pay you. The end, thereof, is eternal death.

Are you still hot for God, or you have started backsliding?
Do you find it difficult, to witness to others?
Do you still harbour sins in your life?
Are you still carnally minded?
Do you, as a matter of fact, lack the knowledge of the Lord Jesus Christ?
Are you still a pleasure seeker?
If your answers to these questions are, "Yes", then, you are, spiritually, dead, and you are indeed one of the worshippers in the graveyard church.

Repent of all your sins today, and the Lord Jesus Christ will receive you back into His divine fold with open arms.

Remember, that you alone will give account of your stewardship.

Shun every worldly shame and criticisms. Come to God and He will bless you, mightily.

Take note of this: To be dead without Christ, is hell! It is, even, more hellish to be spiritually dead, without Christ.

He, who, has ears to hear what God is saying at this end time, let him hear.

Remember this fact, that heaven will always listen to the cries of believers.

PRAYER POINTS

1. Let the Holy Spirit fill me afresh, in the name of Jesus.
2. Let every unbroken area in my life, be broken, in the name of Jesus.
3. Father, incubate me with fire of the Holy Spirit, in Jesus' name.
4. Let every anti-power bondage, break in my life, in the name of Jesus.

THE PRICE OF POWER

5. Let all strangers flee away from my spirit, and let the Holy Spirit take control, in Jesus name.
6. Lord, catapult my spiritual life to the Mountain top, in the name of Jesus.
7. Lord, fill me with spiritual gifts, in the name of Jesus.
8. Let heavens open and let the glory of God fall upon me, in the name of Jesus.
9. Let signs and wonders be my lot, in Jesus' name.
10. Let the joy of the oppressors about my life, be turned into sorrow in Jesus' name.
11. Let all multiple strongmen operating against me, be paralysed, in Jesus' name.
12. Lord, open my eyes and ears, to receive wondrous things from you, in the name of Jesus.
13. Lord, grant me victory over every temptation and satanic device in Jesus' name.
14. Lord, ignite my spiritual life, so that I will stop fishing in unprofitable waters, in Jesus name.
15. Lord, release the Pentecostal tongue of fire to burn in my life, in the name of Jesus.

OTHER PUBLICATIONS BY DR. D. K. OLUKOYA

1. A-Z of Complete Deliverance
2. Be Prepared
3. Bewitchment must die
4. Biblical Principles of Dream Interpretation
5. Born Great, But Tied Down
6. Breaking Bad Habits
7. Breakthrough Prayers For Business Professionals
8. Brokenness
9. Bringing Down The Power of God
10. Can God Trust You?
11. Command The Morning
12. Consecration Commitment & Loyalty
13. Contending For The Kingdom
14. Connecting to The God of Breakthroughs
15. Criminals In The House Of God
16. Dealing With Hidden Curses
17. Dealing With Local Satanic Technology
18. Dealing With Satanic Exchange
19. Dealing With The Evil Powers Of Your Father's House
20. Dealing With Tropical Demons
21. Dealing With Unprofitable Roots
22. Dealing With Witchcraft Barbers
23. Deliverance By Fire
24. Deliverance From Spirit Husband And Spirit Wife
25. Deliverance From The Limiting Powers
26. Deliverance of The Brain

OTHER PUBLICATIONS BY DR. D. K. OLUKOYA

28. Deliverance Of The Head
29. Deliverance: God's Medicine Bottle
30. Destiny Clinic
31. Destroying Satanic Masks
32. Disgracing Soul Hunters
33. Divine Military Training
34. Divine Yellow Card
35. Dominion Prosperity
36. Drawers Of Power From The Heavenlies
37. Evil Appetite
38. Evil Umbrella
39. Facing Both Ways
40. Failure In The School Of Prayer
41. Fire For Life's Journey
42. For We Wrestle ...
43. Freedom Indeed
44. Holiness Unto The Lord
45. Holy Cry
46. Holy Fever
47. Hour Of Decision
48. How To Obtain Personal Deliverance
49. How To Pray When Surrounded By The Enemies
50. Idols Of The Heart
51. Is This What They Died For?
52. Let God Answer By Fire
53. Limiting God
54. Madness Of The Heart
55. Making Your Way Through The Traffic Jam of Life
56. Meat For Champions

OTHER PUBLICATIONS BY DR. D. K. OLUKOYA

57. Medicine For Winners
58. My Burden For The Church
59. Open Heavens Through Holy Disturbance
60. Overpowering Witchcraft
61. Paralysing The Riders And The Horse
62. Personal Spiritual Check-Up
63. Power Against Coffin Spirits
64. Power Against Destiny Quenchers
65. Power Against Dream Criminals
66. Power Against Local Wickedness
67. Power Against Marine Spirits
68. Power Against Spiritual Terrorists
69. Power Must Change Hands
70. Pray Your Way To Breakthroughs
71. Prayer Is The Battle
72. Prayer Rain
73. Prayer Strategies For Spinsters And Bachelors
74. Prayer To Kill Enchantment
75. Prayer To Make You Fulfil Your Divine Destiny
76. Prayer Warfare Against 70 Mad Spirits
77. Prayers For Open Heavens
78. Prayers To Arrest Satanic Frustration
79. Prayers To Destroy Diseases And Infirmities
80. Prayers To Move From Minimum To Maximum
81. Praying Against The Spirit Of The Valley
82. Praying To Destroy Satanic Roadblocks
83. Praying To Dismantle Witchcraft
84. Principles Of Prayer
85. Release From Destructive Covenants
86. Revoking Evil Decrees

OTHER PUBLICATIONS BY DR. D. K. OLUKOYA

87. Safeguarding Your Home
88. Satanic Diversion Of The Black Race
89. Silencing The Birds Of Darkness
90. Slaves Who Love Their Chains
91. Smite The Enemy And He Will Flee
92. Speaking Destruction Unto The Dark Rivers
93. Spiritual Education
94. Spiritual Growth And Maturity
95. Spiritual Warfare And The Home
96. Strategic Praying
97. Strategy Of Warfare Praying
98. Stop Them Before They Stop You
99. Students In The School Of Fear
100. Symptoms Of Witchcraft Attack
101. The Baptism of Fire
102. The Battle Against The Spirit Of Impossibility
103. The Dinning Table Of Darkness
104. The Enemy Has Done This
105. The Evil Cry Of Your Family Idol
106. The Fire Of Revival
107. The Great Deliverance
108. The Internal Stumbling Block
109. The Lord Is A Man Of War
110. The Mystery Of Mobile Curses
111. The Mystery Of The Mobile Temple
112. The Prayer Eagle
113. The Power of Aggressive Prayer Warriors
114. The Pursuit Of Success
115. The Seasons Of Life
116. The Secrets Of Greatness

OTHER PUBLICATIONS BY DR. D. K. OLUKOYA

117. The Serpentine Enemies
118. The Skeleton In Your Grandfather's Cupboard
119. The Slow Learners
120. The Snake In The Power House
121. The Spirit Of The Crab
122. The star hunters
123. The Star In Your Sky
124. The Terrible Agenda
125. The Tongue Trap
126. The Unconquerable Power
127. The Unlimited God
128. The Vagabond Spirit
129. The Way Of Divine Encounter
130. The Wealth Transfer Agenda
131. Tied Down In The Spirits
132. Too Hot To Handle
133. Turnaround Breakthrough
134. Unprofitable Foundations
135. Vacancy For Mad Prophets
136. Victory Over Satanic Dreams
137. Victory Over Your Greatest Enemies
138. Violent Prayers Against Stubborn Situations
139. War At The Edge Of Breakthroughs
140. Wasting The Wasters
141. Wealth Must Change Hands
142. What You Must Know About The House Fellowship
143. When God Is Silent
144. When the Battle is from Home
145. When The Deliverer Needs Deliverance

OTHER PUBLICATIONS BY DR. D. K. OLUKOYA

146. When Things Get Hard
147. When You Are Knocked Down
148. Where Is Your Faith
149. While Men Slept
150. Woman! Thou Art Loosed.
151. Your Battle And Your Strategy
152. Your Foundation And Destiny
153. Your Mouth And Your Deliverance
154. The Hour of Freedom
155. The Miracle of Divine Relocation
156. The Secret of Progress of Enlargement
157. Breaking the Power of the Past
158. Total Freedom and Deliverance
159. What to do When Trouble Comes
160. Deep Secret Deep Deliverance
161. When the Wicked is on Rampage
162. Discovering God's Purpose
163. When One Door Closes another Door Open
164. Power to Put the Enemy to Shame
165. Victory over Death
166. Prayers to Discover Your Treasure
167. Lost in the Church
168. Ways to Provoke Divine Vengeance
169. The Mystery of Dark Market
170. The Darkness of the Night
171. The Re-Possessing Power
172. The Mystery of Character
173. The Deep Truth about Marriage
174. Pulling Down Foundational Jericho
175. Victory over the Storms of Life

OTHER PUBLICATIONS BY DR. D. K. OLUKOYA

176. The Blood on the Door Post
177. Divine Compensation
178. Your Uzziah Must Die
179. Crucifixion of Poverty
180. Your Turn around Breakthrough
181. Divine Favour and Mercy
182. Watching the Serpents of the Magician
183. Wrestling with Shadows
184. Power against Enemy Oppose to my Shinning
185. Divine Repositioning
186. O God Terminate the Joy of my Enemy
187. Steps to Greatness
188. Deliverance from Multiple Bondage
189. The Tragedy of Stealing
190. Power to Achieve Success
191. The Power of Love
192. My Father Connect me to your Creative Power
193. God of 24 Hours Miracle Arise
194. The Mystery of Water Cure
195. Charge your Battery
196. Financial Deliverance
197. Deliverance from Triangular Power
198. The Mystery of Divine Connection
199. Power Against Anti breakthrough Power
200. My Life is not for Sale
201. Disgracing Water Spirit
202. The Militant Christian
203. The Lost Secret of the Church
204. Handling the Sword of Deliverance
205. Power against Business Bewitchment
206. Power through Fire Baptism

OTHER PUBLICATIONS BY DR. D. K. OLUKOYA

YORUBA PUBLICATIONS
1. ADURA AGBAYORI
2. ADURA TI NSI OKE NIDI
3. OJO ADURA

FRENCH PUBLICATIONS
1. PLUIE DE PRIERE
2. ESPIRIT DE VAGABONDAGE
3. EN FINIR AVEC LES FORCES MALEFIQUES DE LA MAISON DE TON PERE
4. QUE l'ENVOUTEMENT PERISSE
5. FRAPPEZ l'ADVERSAIRE ET IL FUIRA
6. COMMENT RECEVIOR LA DELIVRANCE DU MARI ET FEMME DE NUIT
7. CPMMENT SE DELIVRER SOI-MEME
8. POVOIR CONTRE LES TERRORITES SPIRITUEL
9. PRIERE DE PERCEES POUR LES HOMMES D'AFFAIRES
10. PRIER JUSQU'A REMPORTER LA VICTOIRE
11. PRIERES VIOLENTES POUR HUMILIER LES PROBLEMES OPINIATRES
12. PRIERE POUR DETRUIRE LES MALADIES ET INFIRMITES
13. LE COMBAT SPIRITUEL ET LE FOYER
14. BILAN SPIRITUEL PERSONNEL
15. VICTOIRES SUR LES REVES SATANIQUES
16. PRIERES DE COMAT CONTRE 70 ESPIRITS DECHANINES
17. LA DEVIATION SATANIQUE DE LA RACE NOIRE
18. TON COMBAT ET TA STRATEGIE
19. VOTRE FONDEMENT ET VOTRE DESTIN
20. REVOQUER LES DECRETS MALEFIQUES
21. CANTIQUE DES CONTIQUES

OTHER PUBLICATIONS BY DR. D. K. OLUKOYA

22. LE MAUVAIS CRI DES IDOLES
23. QUAND LES CHOSES DEVIENNENT DIFFICILES
24. LES STRATEGIES DE PRIERES POUR LES CELIBATAIRES
25. SE LIBERER DES ALLIANCES MALEFIQUES
26. DEMANTELER LA SORCELLERIE
27. LA DELIVERANCE: LE FLACON DE MEDICAMENT DIEU
28. LA DELIVERANCE DE LA TETE
29. COMMANDER LE MATIN
30. NE GRAND MAIS LIE
31. POUVOIR CONTRE LES DEMOND TROPICAUX
32. LE PROGRAMME DE TRANFERT DE RICHESSE
33. LES ETUDIANTS A l'ECOLE DE LA PEUR
34. L'ETOILE DANS VOTRE CIEL
35. LES SAISONS DE LA VIE
36. FEMME TU ES LIBEREE

ANNUAL 70 DAYS PRAYER AND FASTING PUBLICATIONS

1. Prayers That Bring Miracles
2. Let God Answer By Fire
3. Prayers To Mount With Wings As Eagles
4. Prayers That Bring Explosive Increase
5. Prayers For Open Heavens
6. Prayers To Make You Fulfil Your Divine Destiny
7. Prayers That Make God To Answer And Fight By Fire.

OTHER PUBLICATIONS BY DR. D. K. OLUKOYA

8. Prayers That Bring Unchallengeable Victory And Breakthrough Rainfall Bombardments
9. Prayers That Bring Dominion Prosperity And Uncommon Success
10. Prayers That Bring Power And Overflowing Progress
11. Prayers That Bring Laughter And Enlargement Breakthroughs
12. Prayers That Bring Uncommon Favour And Breakthroughs
13. Prayers That Bring Unprecedented Greatness & Unmatchable Increase
14. Prayers That Bring Awesome Testimonies And Turn Around Breakthroughs.

BOOKS BY PASTOR (MRS) SHADE OLUKOYA

1. Power To Fulfil Your Destiny
2. Principles Of A Successful Marriage
3. The Call of God
4. The Daughters of Phillip
5. When Your Destiny is Under Attack
6. Violence Against Negative Voices
7. Woman of Wonder
8. I Decree An Uncommon Change

OTHER PUBLICATIONS BY DR. D. K. OLUKOYA

The Books, Tapes and CDs (Audio and Video)
All Obtainable At:

- Battle Cry Christian Ministries
  322, Herbert Macaulay Way, Sabo, Yaba, Lagos
  Phone: 0816-122-9775, 0803-304-4239

- MFM International Bookshop
  13, Olasimbo Street, Onike, Yaba, Lagos

- MFM Prayer City
  Km 12, Lagos/Ibadan Expressway

- 54, Akeju Street, off Shipeolu Street
  Palmgrove, Lagos

- All MFM Churches Nationwide

- All Leading Christian Bookstores

- Battle Cry Christian Ministries
  Abuja Zonal Office & Bookshop
  No 4, Nasarawa Street, Block A, Shop 4, Garki Old Market.
  Phone: 0813-499-3860

BOOK ORDER

*Is there any book written by
Dr. D. K. Olukoya (General Overseer, MFM Ministries)
that you would like to have:*

Have you seen his latest books?

To place an order for this End-Time Materials,

Call: 08161229775

Battle Cry Ministries... equipping the saints of God

God bless.

www.ingramcontent.com/pod-product-compliance
Lightning Source LLC
LaVergne TN
LVHW051155080426
835508LV00021B/2639